T0062785

The Secrets of Love for Women

By Scye Royster

authorHOUSE®

AuthorHouse™
1663 Liberty Drive
Bloomington, IN 47403
www.authorhouse.com
Phone: 1-800-839-8640

First published by AuthorHouse 02/21/2012

ISBN: 978-1-4567-4974-3 (sc)
ISBN: 978-1-4567-4973-6 (ebk)

Printed in the United States of America

Any people depicted in stock imagery provided by Thinkstock are models, and such images are being used for illustrative purposes only. Certain stock imagery © Thinkstock.

This book is printed on acid-free paper.

Introduction

This book is based on my experience with men and how I deal with certain situations with them. These secret tips that I am revealing are to help make your love life easier. The goals of this book are to help you find a lover or to let one go. These tips are very easy to abide by so take this adventure with me and let's begin my beautiful readers!

Dedication

I am dedicating this book to every good woman who has been hurt in a relationship. Longing for that significant other but didn't know how to accomplish that goal. I open up my heart to women who put a 110% in their relationships although they do not get half of that affection from their partner. I'm giving you guys the tools to break up and to find the man you desire to be with. Remember, no matter what situation you are in, you deserve someone who appreciates you and makes you happy.

Acknowledgement

First I want to thank my heavenly father for being an awesome God, and giving me the gift to write. Thank you Irene Carson aka Gammie (grandmother) for help raising me and making me the woman I am today. Thank you Shannon Carson for being the best mom in the world and supporting me. Thank you Scott Royster, for being a great dad and giving me your best opinion when I need it. Mom and dad you guys are awesome! Look you guys gave birth to an author! (ha ha ha). Thank you family and friends for believing in me and my dreams, you guys really encouraged me. Last but certainly not least, big thank you to all my readers!! I have the best fans in the world, and I write for you guys. You guys motivate me and I love all of you beautiful people!!

Table of Contents

How to get a man 1

How to be a good girlfriend 5

How to keep your man happy 9

How to gain trust in a relationship 13

How to break up 17

How to get a man

1. Find your target
Pick your man.

2. Do your hair
No man likes a woman whose hair is never done or messy looking.

3. Dress nice
I'm not saying you have to dress like a model everyday but dress decent enough, so he wouldn't mind claiming you as his own and showing you to friends or family.

4. Smell good
Buy some perfume or body spray and when you go see him make sure you put enough on you and your clothing, so he can smell you. But don't overdo it with the perfume.

5. Brush your teeth
Stinky breath is a BIG no no and carry breath mints just in case your breath is not smelling that well.

6. Wear fitted clothes

You're wearing fitted clothes, so you can show him your curves. But not too tight to the point you're uncomfortable. Clothes that are too small for you are not cute. Also by wearing tight pants, you can get a bacterial infection, so keep that in mind.

7. Play the good girl role

If you're a freak, you can't let him know right off the bat because he's going to think you're promiscuous but if you just want sex from him, throw this tip out the window.

8. Smile

When he looks your way, give him eye contact and smile. It's a little flirt.

9. Speak

Every time your around him say hello but DON'T, I repeat DON'T go out your way to speak because it will look weird and it looks like you're trying to hard to get his attention.

10. Hug

Hugging is a sign of affection, its friendly and it shows you care.

11. Compliment

Boys like compliments just as much as girls. For example, "you are cute", "you're really smart", etc.

12. Random

Ok when you're around him, ask him something, it can be anything but don't make it noticeable. For example, if he's next to salt, ask him if he can pass it to you. Another example, if you guys are in the same class, ask him if he understands the lesson that was taught. Talk about the weather, anything! Just say something so he knows you exist and possibly you guys will spark up a conversation.

13. The touch

The touch can only happen in crowded places or if he's sitting down. For example, If you guys are in a store and it's full of people, touch his shoulder gently and say "excuse me sweetie" as if your trying to get pass him. If he's sitting somewhere touch his shoulder and say hello and keep it moving so he can see you walk away. And when you walk away, make sure your wearing perfume so he can smell you when you walk pass him and also make sure u switch like u never switched before. If you're not sure how to switch or walk sexy, practice it with a friend and ask her/him how it looks before you actually do it in front of your guy.

How to be a good girlfriend

1. Pride

Once you have your boyfriend, you have to take pride in everything you do because your man is watching your every move and comparing you to other females. Whether it's his mom, ex girlfriend, or female friends. You have to be on your "A game" because this is the man you want to be with. Believe it or not, no matter how much he loves you, you are just an option. It's up to you to be that different female in his life, who puts pride in everything she does. Put pride in your career, cooking, cleaning, your clothing, the way you act, EVERYTHING! You have to show your man that you care about yourself. Remember ladies you putting pride in everything, is not only for your man. It's also for you because YOU ARE WORTH IT.

2. Be there

You have to support your man through tough times, decision making, venting, etc. Being in a relationship is a job and these are just some of the duties. You have to create a bond with your man, where he feels comfortable talking to you when he needs someone to vent to.

3. Conversation

Communicating is the key in a relationship. You guys talking will inform each other on how well the relationship is going, what's new in you guys life, what you guys need to work on, etc.

4. Be a sweet heart

You have to do things to show your man that you care. For example, have a cold beer and his food ready for him when he gets home from work, run his bath water, wash his clothes, buy him something you know he would like, etc. When you're doing this, it shows him that he is appreciated.

5. Sexy

You have to keep yourself looking sexy for him. For example, buy some new underwear that you know he would like. Remember to smell fresh, keep your hair done, and shave. You can go get your eye brows done, a pedicure and manicure but those things are optional.

6. Be his Freak

Not to many guys will argue with this tip here. If you and your guy are being sexually active sometime you have to get freaky with him. For example, buy lingerie, put a show on for him, use your tongue for places you know your mother will not be pleased with. Also remember to never go against your morals. If your man wants you to do something and you're not sure if you should do it, it's ok to say no. Only do things you are comfortable of doing.

7. Sacrifices

You're going to have to make some sacrifices now that you're in a relationship. For example, if your friend and your man both want to spend time with you, sometimes you're going to have to put your man first. Your friend will understand and if she/he doesn't understand, oh well! They will still be in your life, if they are a true friend. Your boyfriend however can leave you at anytime he desires. So it's up to you, to please him. Just remember what you won't do, another woman will. When I say that, I mean if you don't give your man the attention he desires, another woman will. But again do not go against your morals, no matter how much your partner really wants you to do something.

8. Be generous

You have to be generous to your partner. For example, pay for the food bill sometimes when you guys go out, clean up after his mess, etc. Don't just do these things on a holiday, try to do it all the time.

9. Priority

Your man is now your priority and it's your duties to keep him happy, as well as his duty to keep you happy.

How to keep your man happy

1. Love

You have to remind your man that you care or love him. From the food you make him to the way you dress when you're around him, shows just how much you care. So make sure when you're doing something for him, do your best to please him.

2. Sexy

A man loves their woman to look sexy. When you go out with him, you have to make sure you look nice because you have to shine from other women. That does not mean, dress like a whore. Dress presentable but sexy. For example, tight jeans, low cut shirt, with heels. Also keep your hair done nice and neat. You can also get your nails done but that's optional but, it does help with the sexiness. Wear perfume. Shave your body, especially your private part, a lot of men do not like a hairy woman. Also, when you go to bed you still have to look attractive. For example, wear a nice fitted night gown or fitted sweats and a fitted t shirt or fitted wife beater. If you wrap your hair up at night with a hair scarf, that's cool. It's not really sexy but your man has to understand that getting your hair takes time and money. Also wear scented perfume or scented lotion to bed.

3. Cater

A man loves to be catered. For example, cook his favorite dish, clean after him, run his bath water, shave his butt (no typo), take him out and you pay for the bill, etc. I'm not saying cater to him every day but do it enough times where he notice. Don't just do it on his birthday or holidays.

4. Freaky

You have to keep your relationship exciting. Buy some lingerie, toys, sex games, try different sex positions, etc.

5. Listen

I know it is difficult to always agree with your partner especially when they are wrong, but you have to listen to their point of view. If you don't let him speak or express his self, he will shut down and become extremely upset. You have to let your man play the dominant role. I'm not saying never express yourself or only let him have a say so, just let him be the man of the relationship and when he's finish talking, you can express yourself. If he doesn't let you speak or isn't listening to you when he's done, you should question you guys relationship. A relationship is a two way street and him not listening is selfish and rude. Have a talk with him when he calms down, and if he's still not listening, write him a letter about your feelings.

6. Cleanliness

Men love a place where they can relax and be comfortable. Make sure your home is that place. Clean your house so your man wouldn't mind living with you, bringing his company over, and even potentially marrying you.

7. Space

As much as your man enjoys being around you, give your man some space sometime. Let him enjoy being with his friends. Don't call him every half an hour to check on him when he's out. If he's watching tv, especially "the game", try not to bother him. An annoying woman is not attractive.

8. Gain his trust

Use my tips from "how to gain his trust"

9. No nagging

I know sometimes we females need attention but nagging is not the best way to get it from our partner because it will just annoy your man. Simply have talks with him about the issues you are having in the relationship. And when you express yourself, make sure it's in a cool and calm manner.

10. Don't change

Once you have your man, keep doing those things you did to get him. Don't change your routines because once you do, your man will notice and he will not like it. It's very possible that he will even leave you because of this.

So if you were that type of woman who did whatever your man told you to do, don't change once you guys get in an exclusive relationship because he's expecting you to do those same things, for as long as you guys are together.

How to gain trust in a relationship

1. Express your emotions

Remind your partner that they are a very important person in your life and you would never do anything to hurt or corrupt you guys relationship.

2. No doubts

Don't give your partners any doubts about you. Few examples, don't take your phone everywhere with you, like the bathroom because in your partners mind, it looks like your being sneaky and your hiding something on your locked phone. Do not hang out with your ex, people you had sex with, and people who have/had a crush on you. It can make your partner feel really insecure and damage you guys relationship because in your partners mind anything can happen between you guys. Some people can say you just have to trust your partner but if you can't stop hanging with those people for the sake of your relationship, your partner is not that important to you.

3. Back bone

Your man should always be able to rely on you. When

they are hurting, you should be the first shoulder they cry on. You can't just be around for the good times. If you can stick it out with them during the bad times it will make you guys much closer because it tells your partner that you really care. If they are in any situation you should be the one to give them your best opinion but when you express yourself, also remember to step in your partner's shoes, be heartwarming and understanding.

4. Be your partners friend

Understand your man likes and dislike. Make sure you try your best not to judge your partner because as soon as they feel you are, they will consider you as just a girlfriend. You want to be more than that, you have to get your man so wrapped around your finger to the point he depends on you and can't live without you. It will be difficult for them, to express their selves to you compared to expressing their feelings to a regular friend. But you have to make him feel comfortable to express his self to you. Many people break up because they couldn't vent to their partner because some people just can't support their partners' needs in this area. As soon as you gain friendship, you guys will grow much closer.

5. Talk to your partner

The more you talk to your partner, the more comfortable they will be around you and it will be easy for them to express their self to you. Especially when they are going through some type of confusion, they will have you for their support.

6. Never let them down

If you say you're going to do something for your partner, you should definitely do it. For example, don't make plans with your partner and then ditch him to chill with your friends. Remember that your boyfriend is not forever and your real friends are. So your friends should understand your love for this person and support your relationship. They shouldn't put you in any situation that would damage your relationship. So you have to try your best to please your partner, especially if you want them for a lifetime.

How to break up

I know it can be very difficult to break up with someone but these tips will help you

1. Ask yourself

Before you break up with someone, you have to ask yourself a couple of questions.

+ Why don't you want to be in a relationship with that person anymore?
+ Are you seriously willing to let go of your partner?
+ Think about the consequence of breaking up. For example, your partner can date other people, you guys probably won't talk or see each other as much as you guys did when you were in a relationship.
+ Can you honestly see yourself without this person?
+ Will you be better off without this person?
+ How will your life be affected without this person?

After you made up your mind that you're seriously going to break up with your partner. Let's begin.

2. Prepare yourself

It can be very difficult to break up with someone, especially when you're still in love with the person or if your partner is in love with you. Sometimes it best to practice what you're going to say to your partner because being under pressure you'll tend to forget things. And then when you forget something you wanted to say, you will be mad at yourself afterwards. You might even be tricked back into the relationship, if your partner's intention is for you to stay in the relationship. That why it is your job to stay strong and do exactly what you want to do, and that is to break up with him. So you will have to deny your partners request on "working things out" because that's not what you want.

3. The talk

You have to tell your soon to be ex that you need to talk to them. Try to have a conversation with them in person, alone. You don't want to break up with someone in front of people because that can be very awkward. But if you have a crazy boyfriend, having a friend around (not really next to you guys but close by) you for support is fine. Also try not to text message or email the person you're breaking up with because it's the principle of the matter but if you don't really care about your ex, than text message away.

4. Break it down

This is the part where you tell your partner how you feel. Those questions that you asked yourself at the top, will help you express your thoughts to your ex. Just remember to stay strong and do what you have to do.

5. Get your things

If you have any clothes or items in his house, you need to get your things that same day asap. These are some reasons why you have to get your things asap. First of all, you don't want to see him for weeks or months because you're still getting your things out his house because it becomes awkward. If he's a jerk, he might have another female at his house just so you can see her when you get your stuff. If he's still in love with you, it will hurt his heart every time he sees you and he might try to persuade you back in a relationship, and if he's crazy he might destroy your things. So it's best you just get your things as soon as you can. If his things are at your house, tell him to come get it. If he makes up excuses not to get his things, then tell him you're going to bring it to him or throw it away. It's just that simple.

6. Sex

If you just broke up with a man, you should try not to have sex with him because sex is a very emotional thing (especially if the man is still in love with you). When you're drunk do not text or call him and say you miss or love him, because you might regret it later on.

7. Stay away

If you guys do not have a child or a business together, there is no reason why you guys should be spending time with each other. When you see him around, you can speak if you want (not mandatory). If you see him with a female, do not embarrass yourself and mention you're his ex because you will look pathetic and jealous.

Notes

Notes

Notes

Notes

Notes

Notes

Notes

Notes

Notes

Notes

Notes

Notes

Thank You

I will like to thank all my reader once again for supporting me and my book, I hope this book helps you and your love life. God bless and stay positive!

About the Author

Scye Royster is from Jersey City, New Jersey. She is the oldest of six females and one male. She's currently majoring in education and psychology. She is a inspirational speaker and she loves to educate and help others.

Printed in the United States
By Bookmasters